Thoughts of a retired mad taxpayer

Thoughts of a retired mad taxpayer

By

Jose E. Vasquez Sr.

Thoughts of a retired mad taxpayer….

ISBN-13: 978-1539198468

ISBN-10: 1539198464

Special thanks to:

My wife who teaches writing classes and my kids for putting up with my harsh ways and antics. I am grateful for the hours spent at the Senior Adult program classes I took and to those wonderful seniors who were my classmates.

American thoughts

As I watch and hear the news I just wonder what so many

want to do

A liar and a socialist for the democratic party

A billionaire two Hispanics for the republican party

Our forefathers are turning in their graves as they see how

we have slid

No longer the American way but the fools are more for the

party

As we fall and get far from the American way I just wish

the Lord will stay

Never thought

Man o man what a way to live

Working, working all the week

Getting pennies for what I give

This is really being meek

Give them notice I want to quit

Want more money is really what I seek

But not a very good education

That would really be my salvation

While in high school I knew it all

Without thinking that was my downfall

If I had worked on my education

Being led by foolish thoughts were my damnation

Now I wish I would've gone to college

That would have given me an advantage

And not this bondage!

Back to basics

In my country that I love, the people are angry this I know

Our country can't survive as it is going now

Democrats give so much away so people will play

The game as I see it is giving us a people who are beggars!

They want it all for free and do not give into our coffers

What they do

The democratic party has sunk so low to keep the people's

vote

Promising all free housing, food, but instead they should

give jobs

A step up with Welfare was supposed to be temporary

But people now stay in the system for life do not work or

pay

The coffers are not getting refilled so soon there will be no

more

With lies and promises of free stuff they keep the masses

on the hook

Staying in power is all they want and tearing our country in

their wake

If we don't get on track and do it soon we will be as bare

as the moon

Our Strength or Weakness

What has made America so strong

Was it gold or silver or maybe just guts

A sense of pride and patriotism

What made us strong was how we united

When everybody just became an American

We were not Democrats or Republicans

Now we have war not like any we have had

A war not for land or people but for life

Our enemy has been brainwashed by the Muslim religion

They will kill anyone not Muslim

Our political parties only argue and argue

When we should be bombing and killing radicals everyday

So I hope you all remember on election day

Get rid of the fools and vote to get a grip

Rock Canyon Dream

As I sit and wait for a bite

I think of life and what I like

Fish all day or fish all night

It's just a dream I would not mind

Spring is here

Short nights, long days we are ready

For what you ask? Why, spring of course

The doves are asking, the rabbits cry out

While the quail just go about

The lizards are searching for food

The beetles dig and are ready to go

Birds cry out their songs of spring

I am ready for the best time with the sun

Time

After 50 plus years we have come a long way

Love has been there all along and here to stay

Some have fun others suffer but not us we have love

We worked to make our life more self-sustaining

We built our house from top to bottom

Now we have a home build by our muscle and strength

Step by step we did our work never stopping as it was ours

Going to hell

As we go along in our daily lives little do we notice or

realize

Our politicians sell themselves and fraternize with some

people not to wise

The people which I am speaking off insure they get the

laws to change for them

While we the people who voted them in get nothing but

more taxes and some scam

The democrats are too free with all our money while the

republicans don't give a damn

Banks and money lending institutions are paying

republicans to screw the people

The fine old adage that we Americans do the right thing, is

no longer for the people

It's to line their pockets and get reelected to continue the

farce of freedom in our country

With money you can get it all! Politicians, Judges and

whomever you want, change the law

But poor fools that worked all their lives to give the family

what was needed just get the shaft

Welfare slaves

Is it right to want the world to be more fruitful?

People have changed and will try to get everything

free

The family is no longer sacred, wanting to help

and get ahead

All the young people want is the easy life hard

work is no longer a need

With welfare and free food for all, there is no

longer the need to work

Families in need forget to return to work, what for

they get it for free

The democratic party has enslaved the people and

destroyed honor and spirit

The good ideas for reclaiming the economy has

turned them into slaves

The inner cities have evolved into enclaves of lazy

people

No honor except the almighty dollar to buy drugs

and booze

Women into baby factories as they get more if

many kids abound

Generations of families who got a helping hand

turned to slaves

Shame on you politicians! Shame on you lazy good

for nothing slaves!

Work

As we get older and look around

we see people just go around and round

never gaining or losing ground

they forget that to get ahead

one must work and use our head

there is nothing free in this whole world

someone's got to pay, so work and do your part

of course that's just a thought from this old fart

Teaching sense

Here we sit trying to learn

Learn to know when to turn

To give help and understanding

This they'll learn and become outstanding

Word of Hope

A word of hope to those of you

Who try and try but never get your due

Channel your thoughts and all of your strength

To do the job the way it was meant

For one can see and you must agree

That deadwood will always be

In time you'll get a helping hand

So you must learn the tree will bend

Don't let them break you, stand your ground

No matter who they send to hound

This is easy for me to say

Because I've already had my day

What is that smell!

I walked towards my workshop and saw that I needed to clean-up my shop. There was a lot of stuff that needed to be either hung up or sold. As I worked I still had that odor that I could not identify. I continued to work and cleaned one side. After a break I started on the other side. A lot of antique tools and old stuff I could probably sell a lot for they were worth a good penny.

As I moved stuff and cleaned out others. I was still wondering what the smell was! I moved the refrigerator and thought I would find something that I would not like but nothing. Well I continued to work and clean. Moving tools and memorabilia from my old job. Thinking of who or what I could get for the stuff I had for years.

As I went to the other side I was taking stuff out, some to the trash and the other to be given away or sold. There was a raid jacket and holsters and belts that did not fit. I jokingly tried some of the belts and laughed when they would not even reach around me. Bullets and baseball hats with different logos from police and agencies that I had helped. We sure collect a lot of stuff without even thinking about it.

Finally, I went to the far side and moved some redwood boards and other building materials we had used for our house. I found two drums with matches in small boxes and match books from all over the world.

I moved an old gun cabinet I have had for twenty years with no lock and no guns in there. I found a package of old, old after shave cologne in small vials that are samples which have been given to me by an old friend that sold perfumes and such. That was the smell that I smelled and could not be identified because there were so many different and together they did not smell as what they

were supposed to smell like!

Follow

He is my child this I know what he does may crease your brow

Things that we do are hard but for others it's simply to do

Parents see that kids are free not blind to what others do

Don't follow those that stray and play the danger road

Stay as strong as God made you but soft to those that love you!

The assignment

Well she gave us an assignment and told us what to do

But looking at what we needed I just thought what can I

do

I don't know what all those technical poetry terms mean

I just write the thoughts that are in my head

Well I write and write what I hear from my mind

Just the thought of doing what she asked was kind of

tough

Because what I hear and what she wanted is not what I

feel

So I write words coming to my head even though it's not

real

So teacher dear please just hear what I wrote and give me

grade for trying

Being me

As I look at what I do and have done in my life

I know I would never get an Oscar or a tony

Probably not even a headline in our local paper

But what I will get is the satisfaction of having done my job

A lot of people hated how I worked and I didn't care

I made a lot of seizures and a lot were drug arrests

I caught a lot of illegal aliens who had hid for a while

Many had no concept of why I caught them or how

But if they had heard themselves speak they would've known

Just a word or phrase they used which was un-American

Sounds of words which showed they were not English speakers

Their language was not English first so they used the wrong sounds

Did I help

In my job I did help people but only when they showed

they were in need

The person who waited all night to get a visa for their

family and didn't

Back again for two more nights and still didn't get one,

those, I would help

Very grateful and almost crying the children forever

thankful

The lady with a car which did not work properly and just

died on the line

The father who had his kids and not able to give them food

while they waited

The ones that walked for miles because they had no

money for a bus

Those I would help! And I did!

You can help too

Sitting here just warm and cozy

Listening to the heroes on CNN

Makes me feel like the world is not at end

For there are people who will help

Help those less fortunate without a yelp

Some have jobs that pay their way

While others just help with love that stays

One may think that we are losing that terrible fight

But God in all his wisdom gives them insight to do what's

right

OUR Failures!

Now to look at what is going on in the world, why don't

people see the truth

The democrats don't see the lying candidates or that one

is a socialist

I can only try to imagine what our forefathers would think

of us today

The American way has changed to the welfare way

I want it free is what they say

Before we would think of getting a job and having wealth

for our labors

Now it seems all people want is to get free stuff but not a

job

Politicians could care less with what we voted for

All they look forward to is to get elected again and again

No longer is the shout of what you can do for your country

It is what you can get from your country but for free

No one wants to join the military service to serve our

country

It just seems that it's the only job they can get

especially for the black or brown skinned people of our

nation

I can only imagine what our country will be like in twenty

years

No longer freedom is our backbone no longer fight to be

free

For we are being forced to have our most hated enemy

In our government, Socialism is communism and that is

true

But why are we allowing them into our government?

We, who depend on Capitalism are being drowned out by

them

I can only think that they have fooled those voters with the promises

No way can we pay for all to live without working, no way possible

We can only help the poor and give a helping hand but only for a while

People now look at welfare as a job, get it free that's for me is what they say

When the people that work are in the minority we will fail and fail big

So Wake Up America! And look at the truth we must change or fall

And fall we will as the freeloaders are more than us

We that work or worked till we retired

Word of Hope

A word of hope to those of you

Who try and try but never get what's due

Channel your thoughts and all of your strength

To do the job the way it was meant

For one can see and you must agree

That deadwood will always be

In time you'll get a helping hand

So you must learn the tree will bend

Don't let them break you, stand your ground

No matter who they send to hound

This is easy for me to say

Because I've already had my day

Let me be!

Let me be set me free

I just want to be like thee

I need a job I need it bad

But please don't stab me in the back

The things I need are but a few

I promise I won't burden you

Well, that was the theme of long ago

But now you know where you can go

Long Ago!

In the town where I was born

Lived some families that I hated and scorned

They took all they had from the poor, even their bread

How I hated and wanted to see them all dead

But after the years we have no more fears

For they are gone just like the steers

Drawn and quartered eaten by all of their peers

I may not have much but I am in touch

And sit in my chair on the front porch

Are you there? We were!

When the request went out we answered the call

We didn't hesitate knowing that some would fall

We all came back hurting some even on our back

Now we need the care and we feel we suffered for not

For to see a doctor we must travel and travel a lot

I just wonder what would've happened if we hadn't

answer the call

So now we ask Washington to answer our call

With so many veterans that live in our area

It is time that we had our own hospital as this is not

hysteria

We want only what was promised

Just a feeling that I got

There is a lady that I know

Writing poems is her show

Taking care of her loved better half

Uses up most of her time as she has no staff

My thoughts go to her so her life will be at ease

For a person who cares so much life should be a breeze

So with the help of God above I send this prayer

To her and her family as only I would dare

Just not enough

Oh what a day I had today

I tried to do what I had in mind

But got waylaid and got in a bind

Fix the truck so we can go

But heck I had no money you know

So I just went home and had a bite to eat

But it was so hot this was not a treat

Drank some water that was really cold

That made me feel really good but old

Heat just saps your strength so be prepared

And not be left dried up and impaired

The shot at the VA

Had a meeting the other day

Actually an appointment at the VA

I have been there quite a few times

But never had met the people that were there today

A nurse who was quite a pro by the name of Day

Took all my info and worked away

The Dr. came after a while

Boy she had a nice smile

Kind of tall like a china doll

She poked and poked on my knee and leg

Then told me what I was going to dread

A shot for now to get the swelling down

Then three more but not now

Now I must wait for a few weeks more

To get those shots which I abhor

Thinking?

Shining light in your mind

An idea closing in your head

Or just a thought that you might dread

Power surges in the brain

Or just ideas trying to escape

What a jumble we all have

While just thinking of the days ahead

Welfare ladies

With the heat reaching a hundred

All we can do is bare it and grin

But what the heck maybe even a little gin

One hundred plus is for tomorrow

So we can go and drown our sorrow

Swamp coolers is what we have

Now maybe refrigerated air we must crave

But at the price we must pay

We must wait and just pray

Stimulus checks we don't get

We're too old so what the heck

But rest assured that the ladies on welfare

Will get a lot more then we will fare

For they don't work only make more kids

So their check will come like on a skid

We should make them get a job

Maybe helping a poor old slob

But alas bleeding, heart America will not allow

For the law to work and get them off the cow

Geese Going South

The geese going south in close formation

The leader honking information

Getting close, don't lag behind

I have the bearings on my mind

We're heading south to warmer weather

Where we'll take time to trim our feathers

We'll play, frolic, and romp around

Until it's time to turn around

Rosemary the Nurse!

Rosemary, Rosemary give me a smile

One that will last for a very long while

Working away I always say

Will whittle away the time of day

You're always working and moving along

That is why the day does not seem so long

So do your job and take care of people

And you will go as high as a steeple

Ticker

When I had trouble with my ticker

We could not get up and bicker

I just did what I was told

Rode the bike and also rowed

My strength will return little by little

And I realized we are quite brittle

A lot of help from Mike and Kim

Kept my cup full to the brim

Now I don't want this, as you know

But exercise is now the flow

We fought too!

I read a story that broke my heart

A little story of men who fought

Who fought in companies, but were all alone

Alone because of prejudice, history has shown

Alone due to fear that they would overcome

We died and suffered like all of you

So why can't we even get our due

The war ended and they thought we went away

And now we can't even get our say

We answered the call, knowing some would fall

Nobody was having a ball!

Search your heart and clear your mind

I am here to stay and get what's mine

Winning

Win, win is what we teach

Never thinking if one can reach

For some it's easy for others not

Cause competition ties them in a knot

We must enjoy and play for play

And not to win no matter what

In every game there is a loser

But don't turn them into a boozer

Let's vote them out!

They spend our money but that's not all

Put us in debt they must want us to fall

Give me welfare, free food, but what else

Why not a job, gets you off your butt, and earn your keep

And you know what? Our pockets are just so deep

Our motto is freedom! But it's not free

We must vote out those fools so they will see

That we want our country to remain, Free

Ode to a Lime

Nice and juicy but sour and tart

I use you to make my tea real smart

Now a lot of people may not agree

But you are the best for my ice cold tea

I use you also for my beef soup

All though not as much as anyone would

You come from far and exotic lands

But only you have the juice that stands

Bells of time

As a bell rings on a cloudy day we think of schools or

churches

But never think of time the bells that rang the hour and

half hour

Did this day and night it was always right

Sure wish we still had them in the town square

So all could look and be aware

They signaled time and other things

They were there for all our wellbeing

Some towns have grown too much

While those that don't well they just go out like a torch

The ones that stay maintain the clocks

So one can hear from far away and continue the tick tock!

I know that this is just nostalgic but it was nice to hear the

clock

Do Not Tolerate!

I hear of the hate that I wish would abate

The man hits his wife, run it's never too late!

But she loves him and hides all the marks

When will she wake up and forget the barks

She needs love and not all the hate

From this degenerate who has excess freight

Loving and living is what she must seek

And quit being so damn meek!

Look in your heart and use all your smarts

Leave him and get a new loving start

Flyby

What a sight and with great pride

We saw our air force fly and fly

Tight formation some real close

Show our colors that are the most

Not news

We tend to listen to what is said

Even if we feel a little dread

But all we hear is such trash

We listen to people who are brash

They speak their mind not what is said

Always giving what is in their head

Why don't they just report what is on the news

Instead of giving what their mind just spews

In all the channels that reports just news

Are really hurting us with their views

Incumbents

Are we sheep or cattle to just walk into the slaughter?

Or are we people who understand and will do battle

As the voting places soon will show how we feel and they

will know

Frustration in our congress? That does just what it wants?

Who knows?

They vote themselves pay raises and benefits that show

They care not for the voter or seniors that I know

Curtail their voting power and kick them out into the snow

Maybe then they'll feel just like we do and I know that

they do owe

So go and vote to get rid of the incumbents they've had

their little show

Pass it on

Having friends and being nice

Is not really a bad vice?

Some are good and some a bad

Just remember the good we had

Now that we know and understand

Let's pass it on to save our land

A Shame

America, America how far you have fallen

So many fools have stolen your glory

They have forgotten that democracy is our standard

Socialism is the new trend these fools have embraced

Our forefathers are twisting in their graves

For democracy is being hijacked

No longer for America but for themselves

ABOUT THE AUTHOR: Jose E. Vasquez Sr. is a retired U.S. Customs supervisor who spend his adult life doing police work in the military and his civilian jobs. He is an avid fisherman and writer of poetry and short stories. Jose feels that he has much to write about with all his experiences, but it would take hundreds of pages to tell all. A lot of funny stuff but also a lot of them not.

www.ingramcontent.com/pod-product-compliance
Lightning Source LLC
Chambersburg PA
CBHW060229290526
45789CB00003B/1471